HELP IS ON THE WAY FOR:

Word Skills

Written by Marilyn Berry
Pictures by Bartholomew

CHILDRENS PRESS ™

CHICAGO

Childrens Press
School and Library Edition

Executive Producers: Ron Berry and Joy Berry
Editors: Susan Mustaine and Theresa Tinkle
Consultants: Patricia Harrington and Terie Snyder
Design: Abigail Johnston
Typesetting: Curt Chelin

ISBN 0-516-03243-7
Copyright © 1985 by Marilyn Berry
Living Skills Productions, Fallbrook, CA
All rights reserved.
Printed in the United States of America

So you need to improve your **word skills**!

Hang on! Help is on the way!

If you are having a hard time

- putting your thoughts into words,
- understanding what you read, or
- understanding what others say . . .

. . . you are not alone!

Just in case you're wondering...

...why don't we start at the beginning?

What is a Word?

A word is one or more spoken sounds that have meaning. A word can also be the symbols that stand for the spoken sound. Words, whether written or spoken, are the labels we use to communicate our thoughts and feelings.

What is a Vocabulary?

A vocabulary is a collection of words that are used by a group or an individual. Your vocabulary is made up of all the words you understand and use to communicate with others.

Why are Word Skills Important?

Word skills will help you build a bigger and better vocabulary. When you have built a strong vocabulary, you will

• understand more of what you read.

• understand more of what others say.

Word skills also help you to put better labels on your thoughts and feelings. This helps you to communicate your true thoughts and feelings to others.

Developing good word skills and building a strong vocabulary can be fun and rewarding. The key is to take it one step at a time.

Step One: Using the Tools

There are three books that can help you build your vocabulary:

- A dictionary
- A thesaurus
- A special book of synonyms, antonyms, and homonyms

These books are available in paperback and in junior editions. If possible, you should include these books among your study tools at home. If not, you will find them at your library.

The Dictionary

Many people think that a dictionary is useful only for finding the meaning of a word. Although word meanings are important, they are only a small part of the wealth of information a dictionary offers. Here is a list of some of the other information you can find when you look up a word in a dictionary:

- The correct spelling
- The correct pronunciation
- The part of speech the word is
- Examples of how the word is used
- Other forms of the word
- Additional meanings
- Origin or history of the word
- An illustration
- Synonyms

CORRECT
PRONUNCIATION

PART OF
SPEECH

CORRECT
SPELLING

MOST COMMON
MEANING

ADDITIONAL
MEANING

'pet \ 'pet \ n 1. : a tame animal
kept for pleasure rather than for
use 2: a person who is treated
with special kindness ⟨teacher's pet⟩

PART
OF
SPEECH

EXAMPLE

²pet *adj* 1: kept or treated as a pet
2: showing fondness ⟨a pet name⟩

FAVORITE

³ pet *vb* pet·ted, pet·ting : to stroke
or pat gently or lovingly

OTHER
FORMS

SYNONYM

Pet   ILLUSTRATION

13

Using Your Dictionary

For the most part, dictionaries provide the same type of information and arrange the information in the same way.

- Words are listed in alphabetical order.
- There are guide words at the top of each page to help you locate a word quickly and easily.

To get the most out of your dictionary, you need to know how to find information in it and how to use it for building your vocabulary.

Get to know your dictionary. Each dictionary is slightly different in the symbols that it uses and in how it presents the information for each word. You need to take some time to study the information at the front of the book. Pay close attention to

- the instructions for using the dictionary,
- the key to the symbols and abbreviations, and
- the pronunciation guide.

Look at all the meanings for each word. Don't stop with the first meaning. Read them all, along with the examples of how the word is used. This will build your vocabulary by showing you several uses for one word.

Look at the other forms of the word. You can add several words to your vocabulary by learning all the different forms of one word. Many times they are listed at the beginning or end of the entry. You can also look at the entry words directly above and below the word. Many times several words in a row will be related.

Use the synonyms. A synonym is a word that has the same or almost the same meaning as another word. A dictionary will often use a synonym to define a word. You can add words to your vocabulary by

- looking up the synonym in the dictionary to find its exact meaning, and by
- comparing the two words to see how they are the same and how they are different.

The Thesaurus

A thesaurus is a collection of words that are grouped together according to their meanings. When you look up a word in a thesaurus, you will usually find
- a list of synonyms, or words that are similar in meaning;
- the part of speech, or how the word is used; and
- a sample antonym, or word that is the opposite in meaning.

Using Your Thesaurus

Your thesaurus will probably follow one of two different forms.

- In one form the words are listed in alphabetical order with guide words given at the top of each page.
- In the other form the words are listed in an index in alphabetical order.

Once you learn to use your thesaurus, you will find that it can help you build your vocabulary.

Get to know your thesaurus. You will need to know which form your thesaurus uses. You will also want to learn what symbols are used and how the information for each word is presented. You will get the most out of your thesaurus if you study the information at the front of the book. Pay close attention to

• the instructions for using the thesaurus, and
• the key to the symbols and abbreviations.

Use your thesaurus when you have a thought but you cannot think of a word to express it exactly. Look up a word with similar meaning and search the synonyms for the exact word you want. Look closely at all the synonyms. You may be able to use them in the future.

Use your thesaurus when you want to find a word that expresses your thought better than the word you have in mind. Look up the word you are thinking of and search the synonyms for a better word.

The Special Book
of Synonyms, Antonyms, and Homonyms

This book is very similar to a thesaurus. However, there are some differences.

- This book usually offers more antonyms for each entry.
- This book has a section that includes a complete list of homonyms. Homonyms are words that sound alike but have different spellings and meanings.

Learning to use this kind of book will help you build your vocabulary.

Using Your Book of Synonyms, Antonyms, and Homonyms

This book is usually divided into two sections:

- The first section includes a list of words in alphabetical order. Each entry is followed by a list of synonyms and a list of antonyms.
- The second section is a list of homonyms that are arranged in alphabetical order. Each set of homonyms is listed and defined so that you can see what each word means and how they are different.

Step Two: Reading

One of the easiest and most enjoyable ways to build your vocabulary is to read, read, read.

- Reading exposes you to new words.
- Reading teaches you the meanings of new words.
- Reading shows you how a word can be used in a variety of ways.

There are two ways that reading can help you build your vocabulary.

1. Some reading materials present new words and provide you with the meanings of the words. The meaning is usually explained
• within the material itself, or
• in a glossary at the back of the book.

2. Some reading materials present new words, but the meanings of the words are not obvious. By using the *context*, the sentences around a word, you can sometimes figure out its meaning.

Be an Active Reader

You will be sure to add new words to your vocabulary if you become an active reader. Try following these tips as you read:

- Keep a pencil and a piece of paper handy.
- Write down new words and the page number they are on as you read.
- When you have finished reading, look up the new words in the dictionary.
- Go back in the reading material to the passage where you found the word.
- With the meaning in mind, see how the word is used.

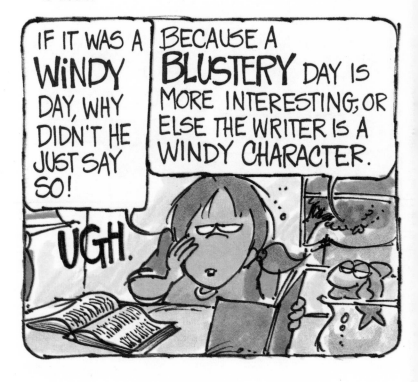

Step Three: Learning the Word Parts

Some words are made up of smaller parts. These parts fall into three categories:

- Root words (sometimes called base words)
- Prefixes
- Suffixes

You can add many new words to your vocabulary by learning about word parts.

Root Words

One meaning for *root* is *the foundation of something*. A root word is a foundation or word upon which you can build other words. *Graph* is an example of a root word. *Graph* basically means something written. By adding other word parts to the root word *graph*, you can create many words that are related in some way to writing:

tele<u>graph</u>   para<u>graph</u>   auto<u>graph</u>   <u>graph</u>ics

A group of words that are created from the same root word is sometimes called a *word family*. A fun way to add words to your vocabulary is to learn all the words in a word family.

- Keep a list for each word family.
- When you discover a new word that belongs to a word family, add it to that list.
- Make a note of how the words are the same and how they are different.

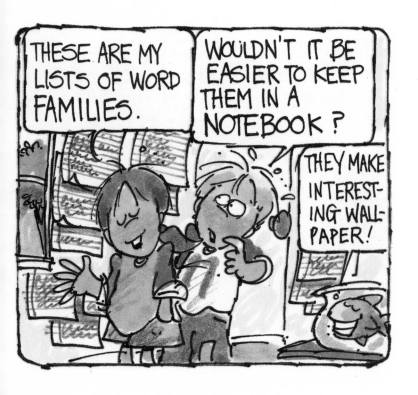

Prefixes

A prefix is another word part. It is added to the beginning of a root word. When you add a prefix to a word, it changes the meaning of the word. *Un* is an example of a prefix. It means *not*, so it changes the root word to meaning the opposite of its original meaning. Here are some examples:

<u>un</u>able   <u>un</u>easy   <u>un</u>clear
<u>un</u>important   <u>un</u>even   <u>un</u>known

There are many different prefixes. Here are just a few, together with their meanings:

bi–two   re–again   sub–under   dis–opposite
pre–before   mis–wrong

You can add to your vocabulary by keeping a list of prefixes. When you come across a new prefix, add it to your list. Write down the meaning of the prefix and at least one word that uses it.

Suffixes

A suffix is a word part that is added to the end of a root word. When you add a suffix to a word, it can affect
- the meaning of the word, or
- how the word is used.

Suffixes and Word Meaning

Sometimes a suffix will alter the meaning of a word. For instance, the suffix *less* means *without*. When you add *less* to the end of a word, the word takes on a new meaning. For example:

- *worth* means *value*
- *worthless* means *without value*.

Suffixes and Word Use

Most of the time a suffix determines how a word will be used. A suffix can change a word into a noun, a verb, an adjective, or an adverb.

Here are some examples:

To make <u>short</u> a verb, add <u>en</u>: I will <u>shorten</u> my speech.

To make <u>entertain</u> a noun, add <u>ment</u>: We need some <u>entertainment</u>.

To make <u>rain</u> an adjective, add <u>y</u>: It was a cold and <u>rainy</u> day.

To make <u>final</u> an adverb, add <u>ly</u>: He was <u>finally</u> learning about suffixes.

There are two ways in which word parts can help you build your vocabulary.

1. Take words apart. When you understand word parts and learn what the different prefixes, root words, and suffixes mean, you can often figure out the meanings of many words.

2. Put words together. When you know what prefixes, root words, and suffixes mean, you can put them together to form new words. When you make up a new word, look it up in the dictionary to see if it really exists.

Tricks of the Trade

Here are two fun activities that can help you build your vocabulary.

Make a Vocabulary Notebook

A vocabulary notebook can help you add more words to your vocabulary and keep track of your progress at the same time.

You can have a notebook especially for your vocabulary, or you can set aside a section in your school notebook. In your notebook you can include

- new words you want to learn how to use properly;
- new words you have already learned how to use;
- words you use often, followed by lists of synonyms you can use as substitute words; and
- lists of prefixes, suffixes, and word families you have learned.

Learn a New Word Every Day

Another fun way to build your vocabulary is to learn a new word every day. It is easy to do with the help of flash cards.

- On one side of a 3" × 5" card, write the word and its correct pronunciation. Be sure to spell the word correctly.
- On the other side, write the meaning and a sentence using the word.

Keep the card with you all day and study it when you can.

Use your new word. Make a point to use the word several times throughout the day.

- Use it while talking to other people.
- Use it, if possible, in your writing. For example, use it in your schoolwork or in personal letters.

Get the most out of your new word. Look up the word in your thesaurus or special book of synonyms, antonyms, and homonyms.

- Write down other words with similar meanings.
- Write down words that have opposite meanings.

Words can become a fun hobby. You can
- collect them,
- play games with them,
- take them apart,
- put them together, and
- share them.

If you try the ideas in this book, you will probably learn many new words...

...and have fun doing it!

THE END

About the Author

Marilyn Berry has a master's degree in education with a specialization in reading. She is on staff as a creator of supplementary materials at Living Skills Press. Marilyn and her husband Steve Patterson have two sons, John and Brent.